T0381340

The Eagle

That Refused To Dance With

Chickens

This is a simple metaphor drawn from African traditional oral literature aimed at inspiring children to build self-esteem and character.

ELIJAH NGUGI

To order additional copies of this book, contact:
Xlibris
844-714-8691
www.Xlibris.com
Orders@Xlibris.com

ISBN: Softcover   978-1-4535-1070-4
            Hardcover   978-1-4535-4090-9
            EBook   979-8-3694-1355-5

Print information available on the last page

Rev. date: 12/14/2023

Notes From the Author to Teachers/Parents

The Eagle That Refused to Dance with Chickens is a story that is traditionally narrated in two African languages, Kiswahili and Kikuyu. This story in particular, although it has been modified to a great extent, is popular among the Kikuyu people who live in the central part of Kenya where it is believed to have originated. The author has worked painstakingly to allow the same descriptive words and phrases in Kikuyu to be translated in English as verbatim as possible to fit in the story. Such endeavor is an attempt to bring the authentic texture of the story as much as possible to the Western-world mind-set. Both the content and style of narration are aimed at addressing issues of late childhood and teen years, thus eight to fourteen years of age. It seems to fit such application because this is the time that children are intensely obsessed in searching for self-independence and identity. Nevertheless, the story has been used as an allegory and adjusted to be applicable to all ages depending on the purpose and circumstances. Quite often, it is also presented as a drama or acted by children as one of the activities that would bring the meaning into the real life of the children.

African Wisdom in Storytelling

When reading African stories, one cannot help but discover the major attributes reflected in the African culture and the richness of oral literature. Although almost every ear in the world hears the echoes of the African drums, few have heard the echoes of the voices of African storytellers at the twilight. Few have known the heritage of African wisdom through storytelling that has been passed on to many cultures in the world, including America. There is likelihood that some of the stories you have heard from your childhood might have come from Africa; for example, the story *Cry Wolf* translated from *The Lad Shepherd and the Leopard*.

Oral literature means that the stories are all banked in the mind of the people of that particular community and then narrated orally, or rather by mouth, but passed on from one generation to generation. This means stories are starched in the invisible libraries that are built within the histories and custom practices of the people. It is no wonder that there seems to be a universal belief in Africa that the older the person, the higher the chances that he or she possesses enormous amount of historical wealth and cultural experiences. Hence, respect is accorded to the older individuals, honoring them as living libraries that seem to give the society an assurance of continuous traditional virtues.

Like any other society, the oral literature does not only bare historical content for a particular society but also as a medium of distributing invisible laws and order. Oral literature then caters for comprehensive needs of collective society yet tailored to meet the individuals' needs in different phases of life, age, or in different circumstances. Some of the elements that oral literature cater for among the many are social justice, love, courtship and marriage, social skills, children rearing, relationship, festivities, celebrations and seasons, grief, shame, guilt, self-determination, worshiping, code of ethics, and even overcoming trauma of any life-catastrophic events.

Whether it is a political, social gathering or motivating contemporary professionals, or communicating to the younger generation, oral literature attributes are greatly valued in African societies. Whenever storytelling is utilized, the orator then must choose the wording in masterly and personalized artistry, making sure the entire meaning and the purpose of the story fit the theme and intended objective. For example, *The Eagle that Refused to Dance with Chickens* is a story full of dramatic events interlocking each other, yet very simple. The storyteller then must lead the listener to widen his or her imaginations and capture the story's characters almost in a literal manner. The storyteller, therefore, must be resourceful in applying adjectives, verbs, and adverbs appropriately in order to give the characters in the story great value in their role; for example, phrases such as "The hungry hyena aggressively jumped on the back of the vulnerable calf" or "With courage, Samba cunningly eased his small body under the belly of the violent hippo."

The storyteller must be skillfully able to design his genre with intonation, pauses that help the listener to experience the atmosphere of the event in different turns, suspense, and dramatic thrills of the story. Poetry, singing, drumming, or dancing, in some cases, are used as interludes but primarily as tools to engage the mind of the child to the theme and in intended teaching in the story. In other occasions, proverbs could be used as concise introduction, or rather, the theme of the story, or as a conclusion line. For example, "Victory is not determined by the physique but through determination and wisdom of planning," or "He who does not listen to his mother will listen to the unforgiving world." It is essential to remember that there is one universal natural dynamic in African storytelling: all stories have sublime meanings and purposes.

It Was a Movie

It feels like yesterday when my heart used to leap with joy when my mother said to me, "Tomorrow is your turn to visit your grandparents." The visitation to my grandparents' house was awaited with gladness and enormous anticipation by all my brothers and sisters. We all would take turns. Sometimes only one or two of us were allowed to visit. To me it was a special day. I knew it was a moment to sit down at the fireplace, wait for the food to cook, and listen to the voice that delivered oral literature like a movie. My grandmother was the principal storyteller in our family. Her voice seemed to have the ability to call the past to the moment or even sending current moment to the mysterious past, yet making sure that the characters in the stories are brought to life and real. Her verbal skills to narrate oral literature were so dramatic that she gently walked our minds into suspense, break into an interlude—singing—then siphon our curiosity back to the theme of the story in great ease without losing attention from any one of us. The thrilling portion of the story provided us an experience similar to that in contemporary movie theater. Almost in every storytelling session, there was always a different one throughout my childhood. My grandparents and parents were my no-ending "blockbuster," or rather, new releases. Quite often, some stories were repeated because some of us requested, or if the parent thought it would be applicable to an event that was current. When there was a lot of entertainment in the stories, there followed some questions that were aimed at making sure the metaphoric characteristic of the story was not lost, and the children have grasped the real-life application of the story. Sometimes we would be told to retell the story in our own words or simply paraphrase it entirely.

There is no doubt that oral literature helped the children to expand their memories, improve children's analytical thinking, and above all, improves the ability to articulate their histories. In my view, it is oral literature that brought every child into the world of culture, social skills, and customs as the conscience and moral principles were being engraved into the child's spirit with fun and excitement. Such practices greatly helped the families bond together while cultivating communal thinking and means to help the children grow with a sense of belonging and identity. It became a tool that helped the village to raise the child, and in turn, the child rises to build the village. The book in your hands now has been written by one of those children; enjoy it as you help a child grasp the treasure of wisdom in the story.

The Eagle That Refused to Dance with Chickens

Sweet Home

Long time ago, in the forest of Mount Kenya, Africa, a family of eagles had a son who was strong and beautifully feathered. His parents named him Ngugi. The name *Ngugi* means "determined leader" or simply "hardworking one." The father eagle was also an honorable leader who worked hard to lead the eagles in different activities that kept the forest safe and peaceful. His name was Mugambi, meaning "the one with a voice of authority to lead." Unlike any other birds, he was able to soar so high in the sky where no one in the jungle could see him anymore. This gave him keen understanding of the weather or any threatening changes. He was dedicated in warning all the birds of the jungle whenever there were any dangers of fire, violent storms, dangerous winds, or drought. His quality of leadership earned him respect from all birds of Mount Kenya jungle. He was zealously determined to raise his son Ngugi the same way. His wife Kawira, meaning "a diligent worker," joined her husband in all efforts of leadership but mostly making sure they both brought up their son as a young eagle of great virtues and character.

The family's nest was built on top of one of the tallest and huge trees that grew on the high slopes of the mountain. From this high place, the eagle family could enjoy the scenery, which was full of natural beauty and wild wonders. The family was able to see far and wide while enjoying the natural vegetation and basking under the cool sun of the equator. Breeze from here seemed to sooth everything with quietness. Behind the eagles' home, on the top of Mount Kenya, is an icy curtain of three snowy peaks that stood like giants of crystals in king's pallor. Below the nest were wonders of flowers that seemed to be hugging the curves of the entire valley. The abundance of flower species adorned the surroundings with every imaginable color. At dawn, these flowers filled the entire area with tropical aroma, and at dusk the petals seemed to wave all animals good night. On each side of the eagles' nest are mass of equatorial flower-vines draping like sheers filtering the sun rays from the sunrise to sun down. The calm river, Tigithi, navigated its clear waters in a path that seemed to be asking every flower of the valley to have a sip no matter how much or how many times. Under the shade of the jungle, the river flowed with ease and elegance that made eagles say, "The river waited to greet the sun in the morning and yet lingered to talk to the moon at night." The river waters stayed cold because it dripped from the snowy peaks of the mountain. It's clear, lazy waters invited the eyes to the deep bed of the river that was decorated with black volcanic pebbles. From the treetop, every eye could see the schools of tilapia and eels enjoying their natural habitat as they swam in peaceful sequences. The whole beauty of the eagles' home was ornamented with huge, tall volcanic rocks that stood like monuments underneath the branches that held the eagles' nest. It is this place filled with wonders of natural landscape the eagle family called home. The father eagle knew this was a perfect place to raise his family.

Word of Wisdom from the Father

Every day, before the father and the mother went out to search for food, they reminded their son-eagle about the dangers of the forest. "Ngugi," the father said, "life in the jungle is great and wonderful. It is full of excitement and joy of freedom. However, you will have to be watchful and stay away from many unseen dangers of the mysterious jungle." Sometimes the father eagle would spread his wings over the shoulders of his son and continue to say, "Rule number 1, never rattle the nest when your father and mother are not at home. Such an act might alert some enemies who would be curious to destroy you. Rule number 2, you shall never try to spread your wings while flapping them in the nest. This might loosen the pillars of the nest, risking your life by falling into the deep sharp rocks of the steep cliffs. Rule number 3, stay within the nest quietly and still but constantly watch who comes around the nest. This will help you to know who can harm you, or the one who cannot."

The father paused for a moment, cleared his throat, and with a low voice, continued to say, "Remember those words and you will be free from harm when we are away. Should you see, feel, or hear any danger, all that you will need is to alarm me with a strong shrilling sound of an eagle when in distress, like this, *shreeeeeuh* and I will hear you. Then I will come and rescue you." Ngugi nodded his head with a smile of assurance and encouragement.

The words from his father made him feel confident and assured. It also made him joyful to know how much his father loved him, and how committed he was to keep him safe.

The father cleared his throat once again and continued to say, "However, the time will come when you will be able to face the dangers of life all by yourself." The father knelt down and looked more stunningly into his son's eyes and continued to say, "That time, you will be able to spread your wings as wide as you can. You will have great strength to rattle your nest as hard as you can. You will be able to do so with strength and with smooth strokes. You will not fear any threat. Speedily, you will be able to thrust your strong body into the elegant sky, and higher you will fly. Your silky feathers will help you swim through the waves of the African winds, and with confidence you will soar high, mounting onto the air with majesty! Your wide strong wings will give you agility to maneuver yourself to avoid danger and conquer the forces of violent storms. When you shall be way high in the sky, you will have a vision of what is far and near. This will help you make better judgment of danger and decisions of now and of the future because eagles are uniquely created, whose spirit of endurance and courage never ceases. It is these abilities that will help you see what others do not see. Always remember you are an eagle."

Defiant Thinking

Several months went by and Ngugi was growing bigger, full of vigor and majesty. The feathers on his wings continued to grow longer, beautiful, and decorated with attractive colors. Some feathers grew gold orange, and others were snowy white, while others were silk grey spotted with soft black. One morning, the father and mother eagle had just left the nest in search for food. The weather was beautiful, and the equator sun shone magnificently. The sun rays reflected the glassy peaks of Mount Kenya like dimmed floodlights. The sky was clear blue, and the wind was calm. The whole jungle felt peaceful, and no danger seemed to threaten. All that you could hear was the soothing sound of the African bees in search of nectar from the blooming petals of African wildflowers. Yes, it was quiet and serene.

It was at this moment that Ngugi grew curious as to how it feels to soar in the sky, and how it feels to rattle the nest like a big eagle. Ngugi slowly got carried away with imagination and forgot all the warning from his father. He felt as if he had the strength to withstand the risk around him. He started to rattle the nest and spread his wings as wide as he could. He also started to flap his wings vigorously. Accidentally, his right wing violently hit onto the main pole that kept the nest in balance. His imagination and feeling of energy seemed to take over. The valuable rules from the father have been forgotten. Ngugi did not know that he had put himself at risk of falling off. Neither did he know that the stands of the entire nest had started to loosen and could no longer hold him securely. Yet he continued to be carried away with excitement and felt he is no longer a young eagle. When he flapped his fragile wings for the fifth time, the worst happened. The young Ngugi fell off from the nest head-on down toward steep, hard rocks underneath the cliffs. He became fearful and, with all his energy, tried to flap his wings as much as he could. Unfortunately, the more he tried to flap his wings, the more difficult it became for him to gain control. He had never flown before, and never had he ever been out of the nest. Ngugi was in great panic and was extremely terrified. However, in spite of such a circumstance, he managed to avoid dangerous rocks and the scaring cliff. Nevertheless, despite the great effort to fly into the sky, the wind kept on shifting him away from his safe home.

Risky Journey in the Air

After a long distance of struggles in the air, Ngugi got exhausted, confused, and lost. Several times Ngugi came so close to giving up. Other times, he would lose balance almost to fall on swamps and violent waters. Severally, he was about to slam on stony hills. Yet he did not want to make the sound his father had taught him as an alarm in the time of danger. He was feeling guilty, and feared he would be in big trouble. He feared that his father would be disappointed in him for not having listened to the warnings, and not having followed the safety cautions. So he continued to struggle all by himself. The incident was frightening, scaring, and shocking to the inexperienced young eagle. He did not have enough energy to put himself onto a tree, so he just drifted with the wind. When the wind calmed down, he found himself landing on a cornfield of a hunter. At this time, Ngugi was hungry, thirsty, and extremely tired. He said to Himself, "I will find a place to rest for a moment and think how I can get some water or something to eat. After that, I will think how I am going to get back home." Poor Ngugi, he was so far away from home.

Exhausted Ngugi Loses Beautiful Feathers

Unfortunately, the hunter had already seen him landing on his farm. He also had discovered that Ngugi was a strong young eagle who had extraordinarily beautiful feathers. "What an opportunity!" the hunter said. "The feathers of this eagle are just perfect, perfect for the dancing costume for harvest festival of the Kikuyu people. I must do all that I can to kill or catch this beautifully feathered eagle."

It did not take long before Ngugi saw the hunter who was curiously walking toward him. "I must run as hard as I can and hide myself. Surely I am in danger," said Ngugi. He, then, started to run as fast as he could from the pursuing hunter. He tried to flap his tired wings up again on a tree, but he had no energy to lift him up enough into the air. He also tried to hide under the corn, but it was not thick enough to hide him. The hunter continued to pursue the exhausted eagle. Ngugi thought of running near the bank of the river with the hope that the hunter would be afraid to fall into the water and stop running after him. Yet the hunter was determined to catch Ngugi and continued to run after him. Ngugi grew desperate and decided to call his father. He took a deep breath, cleared his throat, and called his father. But by the time he started the shrill sound that he was taught by his father, it was too late. The hunter had come so close and was able to leap aggressively on the neck of the tired young eagle. He grabbed him so tightly and firmly that Ngugi was finding it difficult to breathe.

Then the hunter said to himself, "This is my luckiest day. Feathers of wonderful ceremonial colors have been brought to me by the wind. Ah! Silver grey, snowy white, gold yellow, real black, soft black, Oh! Oh! This is my day. I have found what I have been looking for so many years. When I go back to the village, everyone will call me wonderful—the man who is dressed for the harvest occasion. Then I will dance, yes, dance. I will jump, move my right foot forward and back, step side to side—I mean, left and right—step on the ground with authority and pride. I will dance the most popular dance of the

Kikuyu people, the Mugoiyo. The hunter started to dance, demonstrating his dance with excitement and happiness. Then he paused and continued to say, "Everyone in the village, the young and the old, yes, men and women will call me the most handsome dancer."

The hunter immediately realized he was getting overly excited and needed to act quickly. He continued to say, "Let me find a place where I am going to kill this young eagle and get these feathers out as quickly as possible." Once again, Ngugi tried to shrill like an eagle as his father had taught him. Unfortunately, the hunter had held his neck and legs so tight that the sound was not loud enough to be heard by anyone. Hardly could Ngugi breathe.

Then the hunter took Ngugi under a tree shade and said to himself, "Do I kill the eagle first and then take the feathers, or take the feathers and kill him after? I think I will take the feathers first, and then kill him after." The hunter then started to remove all the feathers he needed for his ceremonial harvest festival. All the feathers from the neck, from the wings, and from the tail were removed. The hunter looked at the eagle and said, "I have a great idea. I will not kill the eagle, but I will take him home with me so that I can have the eagle grow more feathers for me for the next harvest festival."

Dance in the Chicken House

So the hunter took the feather-stripped eagle home. Ngugi was feeling cold and naked. When the hunter reached home, he threw the young eagle in the chicken house. Because the hunter had removed too much of his feathers, Ngugi looked very different and unpleasant to look at. When Ngugi was thrown in the chicken house, all the chickens looked at him with amazement and asked, "What kind of an ugly chicken are you, and where are all your feathers?" The young eagle with a sharp voice of anger and frustration answered, "I am not a chicken. I am an eagle." When the chickens heard that, they jumped up, flapped their wings, and laughed loudly until the hunter came out of the house to check what the matter was. But as soon as the chickens heard the hunter coming out, they all became quiet and silent.

However, for many days, they continued to tease the young eagle and mock his appearance, but mostly because he claimed to be an eagle. "If you are an eagle," the chickens asked, "how come you are here in the chicken house?" Ngugi answered, "I might have lost the feathers, but I never lost the spirit of an eagle, a spirit of endurance and courage. Listen to me. I am not a chicken. I am an eagle." All the chickens in the ban just laughed loudly and sarcastically said, "Yes, we can see that you are an eagle." Then they burst again with big laughter.

Every evening, the chickens used to have a dance. When dancing, they sang a song that went like this:

> We are the chickens—solo
> We are the chickens—all
> We dig the ground with our feet and beak
> Pick the worms and the beetles and eat
> We enjoy the corn from the hunter
> We are the chickens.
> *Kookoorrr!*

When singing, the chickens danced while keeping the rhythm by stamping their feet on the ground and acting as if they were digging the ground and picking the worms on the ground. They danced in a circle when the head chicken went at the center and led the others with solo. They repeated this song again and again almost endlessly. This made Ngugi extremely angry. Before the dance started, the chickens would invite Ngugi to dance with them. However, Ngugi constantly insisted he should not pretend to be what he was not. Many times the chickens picked on him. Sometimes they would pull Ngugi's wings and legs and push him into the dance, but he insisted that he was not a chicken and did not feel comfortable forced to do a chicken dance.

When in deep thoughts and head raised, standing at the corner the eagle said to himself "This situation strikes my mind with deep and disturbing questions. These questions do not only question my deviant behaviors but also about my very existence. These are some of the questions I ask myself; do the golden and white feathers make me an eagle or do such feathers grow out of me because I am an eagle? Or simply, am I an eagle because of the feathers or under the feathers lives the eagle? Do circumstances change the eagle's nature or is it eagle's nature to change circumstances? Does the eagle live inside me or in the mind of others? Does my turbulent past design my destiny or my destiny is re-designed at this moment with the help of tools gathered from my past failures? Who will give me the answers?

Eagle's Stun Voice of Courage

Every day when the dance started, Ngugi would go and stand aloof and thoughtfully try to remember how life was at home. Most days, he was thinking about his parents and his life at the nest when he used to rest and wait for his father and mother to bring food. Although such thoughts comforted him, soon the feeling of shame and sadness would overwhelm him.

All of a sudden, he started to behave differently. Sometimes he would sit at a corner away from the chickens. The chickens would look at him as he raised his neck while turning his ears toward the tall trees near the chicken house. One of the young male chickens felt disgusted by the way the young eagle carried himself amongst the chickens. He charged aggressively to the eagle Ngugi and said, "Look here, sloppy chicken. There is no need of suffering loneliness and isolation just because you pretend to be what you are not. Whether you are a chicken or an eagle, should it matter now? *Eeehy?* Does it matter now?

Simply the answer is no, you are in the chicken house. Come on, be friendly. Talk to others, be involved, become social, and you will be among the people who like to have fun. There is no need of being all by yourself. Come on, join the fun. Let me tell you this, when you join the dance, it seems as if you will be so popular and much loved by all these chickens."

"Listen, chicken," said Ngugi with a loud voice. "Yes, it matters." He looked again on the face of the young chicken and repeated the same words with authority. "Yesss, it matters, if all of us behave like chickens, then who will behave like eagles? I know something has gone extremely wrong for me to be here. I know I have done wrong, but you know what, when the done is done, it is totally impossible to undo the done. However, now the left to be done is to learn from the past done so that greater things can be done. I will not dance, and I will not behave like a chicken." With a loud voice that shook the air of the whole chicken house, Ngugi continued to say, "I know who I am, and I know what I believe. I know what fun to me is. Now, move on, go, and move away from me."

The young chicken felt fearful and intimidated by the voice that was stun and strong. The young male chicken moved slowly away and joined the chickens that were also startled by the strong voice of the young eagle. The eagle moved farther at the corner where he continued to think about his life, his family, and his lovely home way afar at the slopes of Mount Kenya. The whole chicken house was silent. It was so silent it was possible to hear a worm crawling. The young eagle voice made even the crickets' sound stop for a few minutes.

All chickens felt Ngugi's voice was different and started to ask among themselves, "Is it possible that this ugly chicken could be an eagle?" But some convinced others and said, "No no, he is not. No, he is not. How can an eagle be in a chicken house?"

This time, the eagle continued to stand at a corner while his head was raised with curiosity and attention. He seemed to be attentively answering someone and nodded his head. Sometimes his eyes would be full of tears, sometimes full of hope. Ngugi happened to be talking to his father, who traced him with his scent and knew where he was. His father was greatly saddened that the son he loved so dearly lived in the chicken house, stripped of his natural looks, and living without his beautiful long feathers. Even when the father discovered where his son was, he kept his presence in the tree, not known or heard or seen by anyone. Neither did he want his son to try to come to him when he would not have been able to fly. So the father eagle kept eyes on his son, assuring that he was safe. The father knew that his son's wings had not grown enough to fly away up to where he was, so he just waited. After many months, the wings had come back and the strength of his wings had started to be restored and healthier.

Ngugi remembered the words of his father, which went like this: "That time, you will be able to spread your wings as wide as you can. You will have great strength to rattle your nest as hard as you can. You will not fear any threat. Speedily, you will be able to thrust your strong body into the elegant sky, and higher you will fly. Your silky feathers will help you swim through the waves of the African winds, and with confidence you will soar high, mounting onto the air with majesty! Because you are uniquely created, you are an eagle."

Choreography in the Air

Ngugi heard the voice from his father saying, "This is that time. This is the time to stretch out your wings. Stretch out your wings and kick out your legs with courage. Start to fly son!" Immediately, Ngugi did as he was told by his father. He stretched forth his neck forward and spread the wings in a way that the chickens had never seen before. He speedily ran in around the chicken house, and his whole body started to lift up in the air. Five feet, ten feet, and Ngugi was up in the air. Immediately, the chickens looked up in the sky and said, "Surely he was an eagle."

Ngugi, with elegance, flew high with pride and looked down to the chicken house from the air and said, "Bye-bye, chickens. Now I will never be forced to dance with chickens anymore. Yes, now your eyes can witness, I am an eagle."

No sooner did Ngugi go higher in the sky than a big sound was heard, as though a thunder coming out from the tall trees. It seemed to travel at the speed of lightning. Before it could hit the ground, it turned into a big eagle. Yes, a big bird, it was the father eagle coming out from the tall trees with great excitement and joining his son with joy of freedom. The father immediately put himself under the entire body of his son just like a child on the back of his father. Then his father accelerated his speed, with his son on his back, almost vertically toward the sky. He then quickly let his son out of his back and made him come down toward the ground. With such a high altitude and slowness of the son to get in control, it seemed as if he was going to hit on the ground. However, like a well-choreographed or well-rehearsed performance, his father followed him; and at about hundred feet from the ground, he scooped his son by letting him fall on his back again. Like a rocket, they both again shot up back into the air almost a distance of three miles in the sky. Then they both flew parallel toward home. Even though the son did not understand why his father did so, his father explained to him that he was preparing him for a journey home. His father also wanted to know whether he had established confidence on flight and the spirit of endurance as an eagle.

Journey Home

As the father and son flew home, Ngugi told his father how guilty he felt to have not listened to his instructions. Ngugi expressed how remorseful he was. However, his father spread his mighty wings around his son and said, "Now you know, as Proverb says, 'He who does not listen to his parents will listen to a cruel world but with suffering.' However, you are still my son. And in danger, in joy, or even in the chicken house, you are still my son. I am glad you refused to dance with the chickens. Fly, fly with me, son. Let us go home. Indeed, you are not a chicken. You are an eagle." His son went on saying, "Because eagles are uniquely created whose spirit of endurance and courage never ceases." From a distance, the father eagle had signaled his wife to call all the eagles of Mount Kenya and the Nyandarua Mountains to gather and celebrate the arrival of the son who was lost but had refused to dance with chickens. As the father and his son landed, the celebration had already started. Like a thousand horns blown simultaneously, the voices of the eagles could be heard way far and wide in the jungle. The owls, ravens, hawks, parrots, doves, flamingos, cranes, and weaver birds all came and joined the celebrations. Each species of bird danced their style and the way they felt to express their joy. They all joined the theme of the celebration.

"Ngugi is a hero, indeed, an eagle who refused to dance with chickens. He stood strong with integrity and character."

The story of Ngugi, the strong young eagle, spread far and wide in the jungle of Mount Kenya and even in Nyandarua ranges and entire rift valley plains. Many young eagles and other birds learned the danger of being defiant and the importance of paying attention to the words of wisdom from their parents. The story became a lesson for all. As for Ngugi, he continuously apologized to his parents and to his community and became committed to tell others about paying attention to words from their parents and the elders. Nevertheless, the eagle family's happiness of having their son back was always a never-ending joy. Ngugi continued to grow strong and wise with enormous strength of leadership and became a great leader of the jungle like his father.

Class Exercise

1. Can you find another title for the story? If so, what would that be? Give a reason why you have chosen that title.

2. What part of the story do you remember most, and why?

3. What story in your life can you share with the class or the group that seems to resemble this story?

4. From each group, discuss the author description of the home of the eagle family. Name two to three things that describe the eagles' home.

1. Write a short summary about the story using your own words. The summary should be from a half a page to a page.

2. What would be the first lesson you feel, personally, that you learned from the story?

3. What can you learn about character from Ngugi?

4. Do you have anything that you have done in your life that seems similar to Ngugi's experience?

5. Discuss some of the things that you might have heard from your parents that involve safety.

6. The following topics could be a project for group discussion.
Also, each student can present in front of the class what he or she thinks about the following topics:

   a. Honesty
   b. Being yourself
   c. Standing on your values
   d. Being cautious on safety
   e. Each group or individual discusses some of the identified mistakes that eagle made
   f. What are the good things that the eagle did?
   g. What role does the chicken represent that is similar to our lives?
   h. What are the good things one can see of being a responsible father or a mother?
   i. Is there any character in the story that resembles a bully, and if you find one, where is he found in the book?
   j. Discuss in class with the help of the teacher about shame and guilt

7. Vocabularies to be learned

i. Find the meaning of the following words in the dictionary.
ii. Please write a sentence using ten of the following vocabularies.

   a. authority
   b. cease
   c. enormous
   d. anticipation
   e. solo
   f. shame
   g. guilt
   h. endurance
   i. presence
   j. constantly

k. communal
l. majesty
m. instructions
n. cautious
o. acceleration
p. overwhelming
q. utilized
r. choreography
s. remorse
t. fragile
u. overwhelm
v. adorn
w. elegancy
x. mount
y. zealous

8. Make sentences using the following phrases:

a. in spite of
b. despite that
c. no sooner than
d. however
e. nevertheless

Find where they have been used in the story by the author and write them down.

9. Use the following word in two forms:

Character

10. With help from the teacher or the parents, discuss the following:

Allegory
Similes
Metaphor
Proverb
Imagery

11. From the story write ten words that are as follows:

Nouns
Verbs
Adverbs
Conjunctions
Adjectives
Pronouns
Interrogatives

12. Make two sentences identifying two parts of speech you are using.

a. What is the role of adjective in a sentence?
b. What is the role of adverb in a sentence?

13. Find at list five sentences that author has used adverbs

14. How would you describe the eagles' family?

a. Describe how each member of the family plays a role for the good of the entire family.
b. Discuss on how the eagle family was a part of the community.
c. Describe how the eagle family handle crisis.
d. In the story describe what you think about the area that the eagles' family had its home.
e. Find four sentences that the author used to describe the eagles' home.
f. Who was Kawira and what part did she play.

15. Can you identify the questions that the young eagle described as "deep and disturbing?

a. How many questions did the eagle ask himself?

b. Pick one of the questions and discuss what you think the eagle was trying to ask himself.

c. As a group or as individual how would you help the eagle answer some of his "deep and disturbing questions"?

d. Write one paragraph on what you think the eagle described as " whether my destiny is re-designed at the moment with the help of tools gathered from my past mistakes"

e. What are the tools do you think the young eagle was talking about?

f. If you had put yourself in eagles position how would you help him to answer issues on destiny?

g. As an individual have you ever had a moment that you had "deep and disturbing questions". If you did would you feel free to discuss such questions with your; parents, with group or your teacher? If you would not like to discuss such matters with anyone mentioned would you feel free to discuss it with someone else, and if so who?

About the Author

Elijah Ngugi was born in Gathuthi village, in Nyeri District just below the slopes of Aberdare ranges found in the central part of Kenya. From afar Elijah grew enjoying equatorial view of the snowy peaks of Mountain Kenya. He was born among the Kikuyu people and grew in the family of twelve children where Christian principles were well blended with traditional moral values. His father and mother in spite of their devoted Christian beliefs promoted and cherished wisdom treasured in the African oral literature. Elijah expresses the joy of every evening sitting by the fire place listening to a new story daily from his parents and his grandparents. It was like a new movie daily.

When Elijah was a little boy schools in Kenya did not resemble the one in the western world. Schools were never nearby. One elementary school could cover fifteen square miles while one secondary school could cover even larger area. Hence like his brothers and sisters Elijah walked to school for over seven miles one way, fourteen miles a day.

After national exam Elijah left home to a boarding secondary school when he was only fourteen years old. Most of the secondary schools were boarding schools as was common in Kenya, a former British colonized country. After four years of secondary there is another national exam held to propel student in what is called Advanced Level for another two high school years that prepare students for specialization in the university. He managed to be admitted in one of the national schools. In both schools they promoted drama, expressive art and literature.

When he was in high school his talent as an outstanding debater and public speaking talent gave him major positions on both British stage plays, like Othero, Macbeth, Romeo and Juliet and African plays like River Between, Ngahika Ndenda, and Shaitani Mutharaba-ini by Ngugi-Wa-Thiong'o. He joined college in Nairobi and participated in more than eighteen major theatre performances. In 1985 his name became a hit in Kenya when he authored the stage play, The Marriage of Dilemma, a play that dared to dissect conflict that existed between the British-colonial perception and African social concepts using marriage thoughts as a metaphor. Later after college Elijah Ngugi became a major participant in Nairobi theatre to help translate Shakespeare's Macbeth into Swahili and in contemporary English, pronounced as "Makabeti". He also helped to put it on stage for the first time, thanks to Professor Lumbandiri of Kenyatta University. Elijah also participated in a production and as a cast of Man of Kafira a play that was authored by Francis Ibuga and directed by Professor Lumbadiri of Kenyatta University. Elijah's brilliant performance as Bishop Luwum of Uganda won him an award as the best actor of the cast with Nairobi Theatre. The Shakespearian stage performances opened doors for him to be in London and Birmingham theatres in England. With great passion of African traditional literature in 1989 Elijah authored his first Kikuyu book *Ambiriria Guthoma Gikuyu Ibuku Ria Mbere* (Start Reading Kikuyu Book One) Later Elijah worked in *Nations* newspaper one of the largest newspapers in East Africa. He worked as an investigative journalist concentrating in political and economic sectors before he came to United States of America. He credits his inspiration to Ngugi-Wa-Thiong'o his name sake; who has demonstrated self commitment as drum major to provoke African conscience throughout the world in his great social political genres. (Although Ngugi-Wa-Thiongo's novels are found in every university shelves in the world, in Kenya they have been reputed as tools that has changed the social and political attributes of the country)

Now Elijah Ngugi lives in Gastonia North Carolina as a human service consultant and researcher. His main office now is in Lenoir North Carolina in the slopes of Smoky Mountains. Elijah is married to Salina Antoinette Ngugi formerly Salina Antoinette Chester from Detroit Michigan a lady he describes as the closest person of his soul and a true life partner. He has two Children Elijah Ngugi and Wachera Ngugi. He expresses great appreciation to his family that has accorded him patience and love as he has been taking away family precious time in order to have a moment to put African thoughts into literature.

Printed in the United States
by Baker & Taylor Publisher Services